THE *Zodiac Files*

THE Zodiac Files

Sample & Marshall

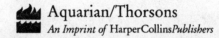

Aquarian/Thorsons

An Imprint of HarperCollins*Publishers*

The Aquarian Press
An Imprint of HarperCollins*Publishers*
77-85 Fulham Palace Road,
Hammersmith, London W6 8JB
1160 Battery Street,
San Francisco, California 94111-1213

First published by Aquarian 1993

9 8 7 6 5 4 3 2 1

© The Zodiac Files Merchandising Ltd 1993

A catalogue record for this book
is available from the British Library

ISBN 1 85538 388 8

Printed in Great Britain

*A*re you true to your sun sign? Are your friends and family true to theirs? All will be revealed. We have collected the very best cartoons so far from *The Zodiac Files* which have brought a daily laugh to the readers of *Today* newspaper.

The Zodiac Files look at life in a star-studded way. Twenty-four characters, twelve male and twelve female, living along side each other, trying to get on and of course, just like real life, not always succeeding.

Each character acts according to their astrological traits so don't be too surprised if you recognise yourself, a loved one or a not so loved one – that's guaranteed.

The Zodiac Files may also help you find some ammunition to fire at the Leo in your life who can't do without an audience or the Virgo who's tidiness is driving you up the wall.

So if you want to know what happens when love-sick Libra tries to wine and dine the butterfly-like Gemini or how a family loving Cancerian responds to a Sagittarius who has a habit of putting his foot in it, read on!

ARIES

A courageous, youthful and energetic individual,
who's fun to be with as long as you can stay the dis-
tance. Any suggestion that they can be quick-tempered,
blunt or easily offended will be hotly denied!

ARIES VIRGO & CANCER

TAURUS

Down to earth, determined and stubborn, Taureans know who they are and what they like and what they like is the good life. They can be led but definitely not pushed, unless of course, it's to a good restaurant.

GEMINI

This joyful, childlike sign is full of good humour. They love to communicate, meet new people and exchange ideas. They also get bored easily so if you want a long conversation with Gemini don't talk about the weather!

Although they appear to be over-sensitive at times, don't underestimate the resolve and strength of this home-loving sign. A Cancerian may not be the tidiest person in the world but they will have everything they could possibly need at hand.

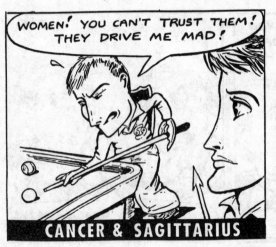

LEO

The King and Queen of the Jungle and masters of all they survey. They are natural leaders, blessed with confidence, charm and the ability to always be right. They believe it, do you?

LEO VIRGO & TAURUS

LEO'S SO SWEET, HE NEVER SAYS AN UNKIND WORD ABOUT ANYBODY

I KNOW...

526

© 1993 CONNAUGHT CREIGHTON-WARD LTD/TODAY SYNDICATION

...IT'S BECAUSE HE ONLY EVER TALKS ABOUT HIMSELF!

VIRGO

Those delightful individuals who insist they are not excessively precise, logical or critical, it's just that everybody else is sloppy. Fastidious and highly intelligent, at least that's what they say. But they would, wouldn't they?

LIBRA

This gentle, diplomatic sign loves beauty but is prone to vanity, laziness and indecision. Their desire for balance and harmony is so strong they will do anything to avoid confrontation. It's not winning a fight with Libra that's hard, it's getting them to start one in the first place!

They are passionate, spiritual and intense as well as being moody, vengeful and tenacious. They make great partners but the sting is would you dare to date one or could you risk refusing?

SAGITTARIUS

This wise, strong-willed sign will always look on the bright side of life. On the darker side they can be reckless and impatient, however, the speedloving Sagittarius knows there is a pot of gold at the end of every rainbow ... isn't there?

CAPRICORN

The sign of the achiever, onwards and upwards, Capricorn will patiently stay the course, especially if it means occupying a position of authority and respect. Being practical they love a bargain but only if it's got the right label!

AQUARIUS

This original, creative sign can be hard to understand, not because they are devious but because they are so unpredictable. They won't stand any pretensions, so if the truth hurts you'd better not ask Aquarius!

PISCES

An oasis of spirituality this artistic sign is patient, friendly and kind. An individual always eager to get to the bottom of your most difficult problems ... and share them with everyone else!

PISCES • *Female*